INSIDE THE NFL

NEW YORK GIANTS

by Charlie Beattie

Abdo & Daughters
MIDDLE GRADE NONFICTION
An imprint of Abdo Publishing
abdobooks.com

ABDOBOOKS.COM

Published by Abdo Publishing, a division of ABDO, PO Box 398166, Minneapolis, Minnesota 55439.

Printed in China.
052025
092025

THIS BOOK CONTAINS RECYCLED MATERIALS

Cover Photos: Sarah Stier/Getty Images Sport/Getty Images (Malik Nabers); Focus on Sport/Getty Images Sport/Getty Images (Lawrence Taylor)
Interior Photos: Lauren Leigh Bacho/Getty Images Sport/Getty Images, 4–5; Gregory Shamus/Getty Images Sport/Getty Images, 6; Michael Hickey/Getty Images Sport/Getty Images, 7; Luke Hales/Getty Images Sport/Getty Images, 8, 11, 63; Sue Ogrocki/AP Images, 9; Kevin Sabitus/Getty Images Sport/Getty Images, 10; Abdo Publishing, 12–13, 58; Bettmann/Getty Images, 14–15, 16, 17, 60 (top left), 60 (bottom); AP Images, 19, 20, 30, 34, 60 (top right); Ross Lewis/Getty Images Sport/Getty Images, 21; Robert Riger/Getty Images Sport/Getty Images, 22–23, 25, 31; David Durochik/AP Images, 24; Robert Riger/Hulton Archive/Getty Images, 26; Hy Peskin/Sports Illustrated/Getty Images, 27; Fred Morgan/New York Daily News Archive/Getty Images, 28; Focus on Sport/Getty Images, 29, 32, 39, 61 (top left); G. Paul Burnett/AP Images, 35; Focus on Sport/Getty Images Sport/Getty Images, 36–37, 53; George Gojkovich/Getty Images Sport/Getty Images, 38; Eric Risberg/AP Images, 40; George Rose/Getty Images Sport/Getty Images, 42, 44; Paul Sakuma/AP Images, 43; Ed Reinke/AP Images, 45, 61 (bottom left); Timothy A. Clary/AFP/Getty Images, 47; Jed Jacobsohn/Getty Images Sport/Getty Images, 48–49; Al Bello/Getty Images Sport/Getty Images, 50; Harry How/Getty Images Sport/Getty Images, 51; David J. Phillip/AP Images, 52, 63; David Duprey/AP Images, 54, 61 (top right); Perry Knotts/AP Images, 56; David Stluka/AP Images, 57, 61 (bottom right); Ryan Kang/AP Images, 59

Editor: Rebecca Higgins
Series Designer: Laura Graphenteen
Production Designer: Ryan Gale

Library of Congress Control Number: 2024948459

Publisher's Cataloging-in-Publication Data

Names: Beattie, Charlie, author.
Title: New York Giants / by Charlie Beattie
Description: Minneapolis, Minnesota: Abdo Publishing, 2026 | Series: Inside the NFL | Includes online resources and index.
Identifiers: ISBN 9781098296858 (lib. bdg.) | ISBN 9798384919377 (ebook)
Subjects: LCSH: New York Giants (Football team)--Juvenile literature. | National Football League--Juvenile literature. | Football teams--Juvenile literature. | American football--Juvenile literature.
Classification: DDC 796.33264--dc23

CONTENTS

New York Giants wide receiver Malik Nabers stiff arms a Cleveland Browns defender on September 22, 2024.

CHAPTER 1

NEW NABERS

THE NEW YORK GIANTS WERE IN A BAD WAY. IT WAS WEEK 3 OF THE 2024 National Football League (NFL) season, and New York was already 0–2. Now the Giants faced the Browns on the road in Cleveland. A loss would all but tank the Giants' season before it could even really get started.

Giants fans had one big reason for optimism. The team's prized first-round draft pick, wide receiver Malik Nabers, had shown promise. After making five catches in his first game, Nabers grabbed 10 passes for 127 yards and his first NFL touchdown in Week 2. Now seeking their first win of the season, the Giants looked set to feed Nabers the ball as much as possible.

At the snap of the ball, Nabers charged downfield. As he broke deep into the Browns' secondary, the wide receiver turned back to look

Nabers, *wearing suit*, entered the 2024 NFL Draft as a top prospect after a standout career at Louisiana State.

for a pass. Giants quarterback Daniel Jones had already lobbed the ball toward his new favorite target. But a Cleveland cornerback covered Nabers and was between the rookie and the ball. Nearing the sideline, Nabers leaped high over the defender's head. Both players reached for the ball, but Nabers ripped it down for a 28-yard gain.

MINING FOR A GEM

All eyes had been on the Giants as they prepared for the 2024 NFL Draft. The team was the focus of the HBO television network's long-running show *Hard Knocks*. Each season took viewers behind the scenes of an NFL team. Fans didn't just see New York's offices and locker rooms. They also saw how the Giants planned to make their draft selections.

After a disappointing 2023 season, New York had the sixth pick. General manager Joe Schoen and head coach Brian Daboll agreed that the team needed an offensive weapon. In the draft, three receivers were considered top prospects. Marvin Harrison Jr. was an incredible athlete whose father, Marvin Harrison Sr., was a Hall of Fame NFL receiver. Rome Odunze had helped lead the University of Washington to the college national championship game. Meanwhile, Nabers had starred at Louisiana State. He seemed set to follow former Tigers' receivers Justin Jefferson and Ja'Marr Chase on the path to NFL stardom.

The TV series followed the Giants for weeks as they studied and interviewed all three players. Many experts expected that Harrison would be the first

Joe Schoen joined the New York Giants as the team's general manager in 2022.

receiver selected in the draft. But in a pivotal scene on the show, Schoen asked Giants' wide receivers coach Mike Groh which player was his favorite. Without hesitating, Groh said Nabers. Like the rest of the Giants' coaches, Groh loved Nabers's combination of elite athleticism, toughness, and competitive spirit.

During the first round of the draft, the Giants waited and wondered whether their wish of choosing Nabers would be granted. The Arizona Cardinals selected Harrison with the fourth pick. When it was time for the Giants' pick, Nabers was still undrafted. The team snapped him up.

Nabers warms up before a 2024 game.

RECORD-BREAKING ROOKIE

After an excellent training camp and a solid first couple games, Nabers looked like a seasoned pro. And against the Browns, Jones continued to rely on his rookie receiver. The 6-foot, 200-pound Nabers responded. A few plays after his incredible catch along the sideline, Nabers got into position on the left side for third-and-goal. On the snap, he broke toward the middle of the field, then back out again. Jones threw a high pass. Nabers was in a tight spot in the corner of the end zone. But the receiver sprang up to grab the ball, then twisted his body on the way down to keep both feet inbounds. The acrobatic touchdown gave New York a 14–7 lead with 1:44 left until halftime.

Nabers stretches to keep his feet inbounds on his first touchdown reception against Cleveland.

New York quickly retook possession with time to score again. With 15 seconds left, Nabers was ready on the left side of the 4-yard line. He sprinted forward, then broke to the middle. As soon as Nabers made his move, Jones fired a pass right on target. Nabers grabbed the ball and hauled it in for another touchdown.

Jones ended up throwing to Nabers 12 times against the Browns. The rookie caught eight of those passes for 78 yards during the 21–15 win. Nabers became the first rookie in NFL history to post at least 20 receptions, 250 yards, and three touchdowns in his first three games. And Giants fans hoped Nabers was just getting started.

UNRETIRED

In 1935, the Giants retired the No. 1 jersey in honor of their star receiver Ray Flaherty. It was the first number ever retired in the NFL. Flaherty's family gave the team its blessing to unretire the number for Malik Nabers. The newcomer responded by thanking the Flahertys, saying, "I understand the responsibility, and I will do everything in my power to honor the Flaherty family and this organization."

Nabers reached the 2024 Pro Bowl as a rookie.

NFL TEAMS MAP

NFC

NFC EAST

- DALLAS COWBOYS
- NEW YORK GIANTS
- PHILADELPHIA EAGLES
- WASHINGTON COMMANDERS

NFC WEST

- ARIZONA CARDINALS
- LOS ANGELES RAMS
- SAN FRANCISCO 49ERS
- SEATTLE SEAHAWKS

NFC NORTH

- CHICAGO BEARS
- DETROIT LIONS
- GREEN BAY PACKERS
- MINNESOTA VIKINGS

NFC SOUTH

- ATLANTA FALCONS
- CAROLINA PANTHERS
- NEW ORLEANS SAINTS
- TAMPA BAY BUCCANEERS

AFC

AFC EAST

- BUFFALO BILLS
- MIAMI DOLPHINS
- NEW ENGLAND PATRIOTS
- NEW YORK JETS

AFC WEST

- DENVER BRONCOS
- KANSAS CITY CHIEFS
- LAS VEGAS RAIDERS
- LOS ANGELES CHARGERS

AFC NORTH

- BALTIMORE RAVENS
- CINCINNATI BENGALS
- CLEVELAND BROWNS
- PITTSBURGH STEELERS

AFC SOUTH

- HOUSTON TEXANS
- INDIANAPOLIS COLTS
- JACKSONVILLE JAGUARS
- TENNESSEE TITANS

New York Giants head coach Bob Fowell, *right*, talks with his team in 1925.

CHAPTER 2

THE NEW YORK FOOTBALL GIANTS

THE NFL'S FIRST SEASON WAS 1920, BUT AT THE TIME THERE WAS nothing "national" about the league. Most of its teams played in the Midwest. Few people in other parts of the country even knew about the league.

Wanting to grow professional football, NFL owners knew that they needed to place teams in larger cities such as New York. In 1925, the league offered a team to New York businessman Tim Mara. Mara had never watched a professional game but agreed to start a franchise. He called his team the Giants. At the time, New York also had a baseball team called the Giants. To avoid confusion, Mara named his team the New York Football Giants, which remains the team's official name.

Chicago Bears star Red Grange, *with ball*, drew fans to New York's Polo Grounds in 1925, which helped solve the Giants' financial problems.

To buy the Giants, Mara paid the NFL $500, which was worth about $8,000 in 2025 money. It turned out to be a great investment for the Mara family. They still owned the team in 2025, and by then the Giants were valued at $7.3 billion. But early on, the Giants were in danger of failing.

An opposing team helped save the Giants. Late in the 1925 season, the Chicago Bears came to New York. The Bears featured star runner Red Grange, who was a national celebrity. More than 70,000 fans came out to see Grange play, and the money earned from ticket sales kept the Giants going.

THE SNEAKERS GAME

Despite the Bears' help in 1925, the two teams soon became championship rivals. The 1927 Giants had one of the most overpowering defenses of all time. In those days, the team with the best record was named NFL champion. And after giving up only 20 points in 13 games, New York finished 11–1–1 to easily claim its first NFL title.

The league's first official title game was held in 1933. Coming off an 11–3 season, New York traveled to Chicago to play the Bears for the championship. Chicago won the game 23–21. So when the teams met again in the 1934 title game in New York, the Giants were out for revenge.

The Giants, *wearing white helmets*, battle the Bears on a slippery field during the 1934 NFL title game.

This time the Giants hosted the Bears at their home stadium, the Polo Grounds. However, icy December weather left the field frozen over. Both teams kept slipping as their cleats failed to get any traction. The Bears led 10–3 as the teams went to their locker rooms for halftime.

By then, the Giants were working on a solution. Before the game, the team's trainer had sent sideline assistant Abe Cohen to get sneakers. Cohen took a taxi to the Manhattan College athletic building, then went into the basketball locker room and grabbed as many sneakers as he could find. There weren't enough for every athlete, but by the fourth quarter many Giants players wore sneakers. The team scored 27 points in the final 15 minutes to win "the Sneakers Game" 30–13. Years later, Bears star fullback Bronko Nagurski said, "They just outsmarted us, I guess."

"THEY JUST OUTSMARTED US, I GUESS."

—BRONKO NAGURSKI

GIANTS IN THE FIELD

A trip to a third straight NFL title game in 1935 ended in a loss. But New York was already rebuilding. After playing for nearby Fordham University, quarterback Ed Danowski had joined the team in 1934. By 1935, he was a star both running and passing the football. He's still the only Giants quarterback to lead the NFL in passing twice. Hard-charging running back Alphonse "Tuffy" Leemans signed on in 1936. He led the league in rushing his first season. He spent his entire eight-year career in New York.

The team's heart was center and linebacker Mel Hein. After joining the Giants in 1938, the two-way star never missed a game

Giants center/linebacker Mel Hein, *right*, receives a watch from NFL commissioner Joseph Carr after winning the 1938 NFL MVP Award.

in 15 seasons. Nicknamed "Cappy" after becoming the team's captain, Hein was a ferocious blocker on offense and one of the game's best defenders. In 1938, he won the NFL's Most Valuable Player (MVP) Award. More than 90 years later, Hein remained the only offensive lineman in league history to earn the honor. That year, Danowski, Hein, and Leemans led New York to an 8–2–1 record and another NFL title game. Facing the Green Bay Packers, all the Giants' stars showed up. Danowski threw two touchdown passes and recorded an interception on defense. Leemans rushed for a 6-yard score. Hein also recovered a fumble. With a 23–17 win, the Giants were NFL champions for a third time.

THE ROCK

The Giants' defense helped them be successful. Steve Owen had been a lineman on New York's dominant 1927 defense. Three years later, in 1930, he took over as Giants coach. The Giants players loved playing for Owen. They also won a lot. His innovative defenses played a major role in those victories.

One of his innovations was the 5-3 defense. At the time, most teams used seven linemen. Owen instead used five linemen, with three linebackers behind them. The coach later developed another

Head coach Steve Owen, *left*, celebrates with his players after beating Washington in December 1943.

defense with four defensive backs to slow down the opposing teams' passing games. Many modern NFL defensive coaches use concepts that Owen created.

The Giants went to the title game four times between 1939 and 1946. However, they lost each one. In 1950, the Giants traveled to Cleveland to face the Browns in a playoff game. Both teams were 10–2. But once again, New York fell short and then had to watch as Cleveland won the title game.

By 1953, the Giants were struggling. The team finished 3–9. Owen resigned after the season. It was a bittersweet ending to one of the longest coaching runs in NFL history. But soon a new successful era would begin in New York.

THE MARA FAMILY

The Maras have owned the Giants since the team was founded. Tim Mara's son Jack took over as team president in 1933. When Jack died in 1965, his younger brother Wellington became president and served in that role until his death in 2005. Then Wellington's son John became the team president. Meanwhile, in 1991, Wellington's nephew, also named Tim, sold his half of the team to businessman Preston Robert Tisch. The Tisch and Mara families continue to share ownership of the team.

Wellington Mara started with the team as a ball boy in the 1920s.

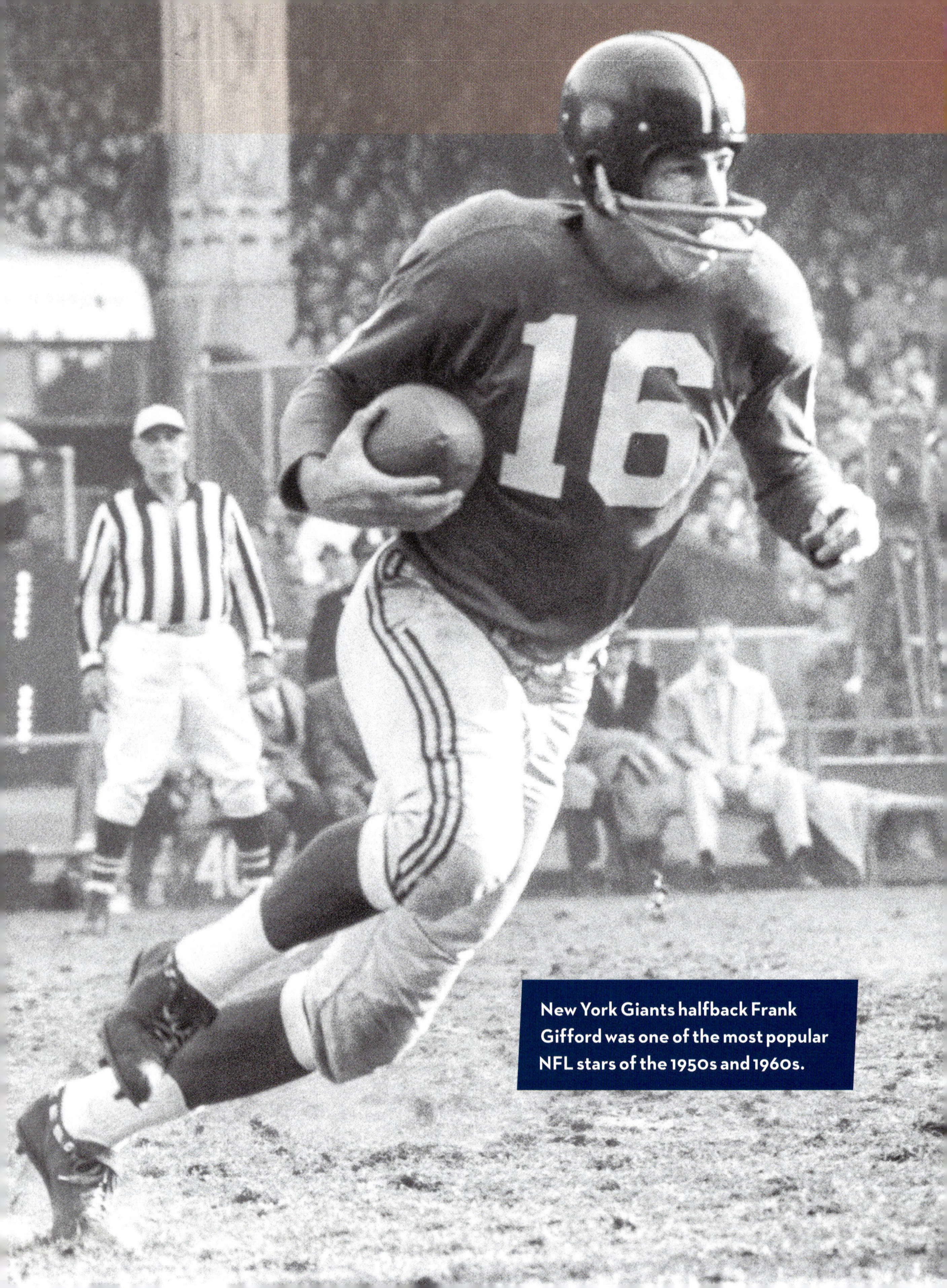

New York Giants halfback Frank Gifford was one of the most popular NFL stars of the 1950s and 1960s.

CHAPTER 3

NEARLY A DYNASTY

THE MARAS APPROACHED JIM LEE HOWELL TO BE THE GIANTS' NEW head coach before the 1954 season. Howell said he would take the job if he could hire Vince Lombardi as his offensive coordinator and Tom Landry as defensive coordinator. The Maras agreed and a legendary coaching staff formed.

On offense, Lombardi unleashed versatile halfback Frank Gifford. In 1956, he led the league with 1,422 total offensive yards on his way to earning the league's MVP Award. And he had plenty of help. Beside him in the backfield were thumping backs Alex Webster and Mel Triplett. In the passing game, quarterbacks Don Heinrich and Charlie Conerly often aimed for fan-favorite receiver Kyle Rote.

Landry's defense had even more stars. Safety Emlen Tunnell was one of the most disruptive

In 1948, defensive back Emlen Tunnell became the first Black player on the Giants. He later became the first Black player inducted into the Pro Football Hall of Fame.

secondary players in NFL history. He recorded 74 interceptions with the Giants from 1948 to 1958. Up front, defensive linemen Rosey Grier and Andy Robustelli stuffed opposing runners. The Giants signed linebacker Sam Huff in 1956, but the rookie almost quit during training camp. Howell, who was always hard on rookie players, criticized the 21-year-old so much that Huff was ready to walk away. Lombardi convinced Huff to stick it out, and Huff went on to become a key part of the Giants' defense. Huff was so successful in the NFL that he reached the Hall of Fame.

In 1956, the Giants finished 8-3-1 and won the NFL's East Division. They then faced the Chicago Bears in the NFL title game. By then, the Giants had begun playing at Yankee Stadium. Just like the Polo Grounds in 1934, the Yankee Stadium turf was frozen when the teams took the field in 1956. This time, the Giants were ready from the start. The entire team came out in sneakers and roughed up the slipping Bears. Triplett ran for a touchdown, while Webster scored two more. Gifford caught four passes for 131 yards and a touchdown. New York won its first title in 18 years in a 47-7 rout.

THE CHANT

In 1956, the Giants were urged on by a new chant from the stands. Whenever the Giants' defenders were on the field, fans at Yankee Stadium began chanting "Dee-FENSE!" The chant became so popular that it soon spread to other teams, and other sports. It is still heard at sporting events.

Fans cheer on the Giants at Yankee Stadium during a game in the 1950s.

THE 4–3

New York's footwear was one reason the Giants were champions again, but Laundry's defense was the bigger factor. Once again, New York cooked up another scheme. At the time, most teams played five defensive linemen and two linebackers. Landry took his middle lineman and moved him back, creating the middle linebacker position. The new 4-3 defense gave the Giants flexibility. While the team still had four players up front to stop running plays, three could also drop back to help the secondary on passing plays. Within a few years, nearly every NFL team had copied Landry's scheme, which is still widely used.

One of the biggest reasons Landry used the 4-3 defense was to stop the powerful Cleveland Browns. New York met its East Division rival for the final game of the 1958 regular season. Cleveland had a 9-2 record, and the Giants were close behind at 8-3. To force a tie at the top of the standings, New York needed to win. But in the first quarter, Cleveland's all-world running back Jim Brown broke

Three Giants defenders try to slow down running back Jim Brown during a 1957 game against the Cleveland Browns.

for a 65-yard scoring run. The Giants responded, and the teams were tied 10–10 in the fourth quarter. Everything came down to a last-second field-goal attempt by Giants' kicker Pat Summerall. His 49-yard kick sailed through the uprights to win the snowy game at Yankee Stadium.

The victory set up a rematch a week later in the playoffs. With a spot in the NFL Championship Game on the line, the Giants completely shut down Brown and his team. Brown carried the ball only seven times for 8 yards as New York won 10–0.

THE GREATEST GAME EVER PLAYED

The Giants hosted the Baltimore Colts for the 1958 NFL Championship Game. More than 64,000 fans watched at Yankee Stadium. But even more important, the game was broadcast around the country on NBC. Throughout the 1950s, football's popularity had been growing, but it was still behind baseball as the national sport.

Roughly 45 million people watched the Giants and Baltimore Colts compete in the 1958 NFL Championship Game on television.

The Giants and Colts played a thrilling game. New York fell behind 14–3 at halftime, but one wild play rallied the team. Conerly threw a long pass to Rote. After the catch, Rote broke two tackles and raced into Baltimore territory. But when defenders caught up, Rote fumbled. Webster raced in, scooped up the ball, and ran to the Colts' 1-yard line. Triplett then scored to pull New York to within four points at 14–10. In the fourth quarter, Conerly and Gifford hooked up on a 15-yard touchdown pass to take a 17–14 lead. However, the Colts tied the game on a field goal in the final seconds of the fourth quarter and forced the NFL's first-ever overtime game. New York went three and out. Baltimore got the ball and drove downfield for the winning score. The exciting matchup rocketed football into contention for the United States' top sport. That game became known as "the Greatest Game Ever Played."

The coaching team of Tom Landry, *left*, Jim Lee Howell, *center*, and Vince Lombardi, *right*, led the Giants through the 1950s.

AIRING IT OUT

Unfortunately for the Giants, the 1958 NFL Championship Game loss was a sign of things to come. The team lost the 1959 title game

Giants quarterback Y. A. Tittle prepares to unleash a pass during a game against the St. Louis Cardinals in the 1960s.

to the Colts 31–16. By 1961, Howell, Landry, and Lombardi had all left New York. Lombardi had taken over the Green Bay Packers in 1959 and was in the process of turning them into the NFL's best team. Landry moved on to coach the Dallas Cowboys in 1960. He spent 30 seasons coaching the Cowboys.

Meanwhile, the Giants let Howell go after a frustrating 1960 season and replaced him with Allie Sherman. The coach opened up the passing game under quarterback Y. A. Tittle. The veteran had come over in a trade with the San Francisco 49ers and began launching deep balls to Rote and new star receiver Del Shofner. With a wide-open offense, the Giants finished 10–2–1 in 1961. In the 1961 NFL title game, Lombardi's Packers intercepted Tittle four times in a 37–0 rout.

Entering Week 7 of the 1962 season against Washington, the 36-year-old Tittle had thrown nine touchdown passes. Playing four days after his birthday, Tittle gave himself a late present. He threw three touchdown passes in the first half. Tittle doubled that total in the third quarter, including a 63-yarder to Gifford. In the fourth, Tittle matched the NFL record by throwing his seventh touchdown as New York won 49–34. By the end of the season, Tittle had thrown an NFL-record 33 touchdown passes. But once again, New York lost the title game to the Packers. Tittle failed to throw a touchdown pass in a 16–7 defeat.

Halfback and end Kyle Rote had 48 receiving touchdowns and 52 total touchdowns in his 11 years with the Giants.

During the 1963 season, Tittle broke his own record by throwing 36 touchdown passes and won the league MVP Award. New York dominated the East, finishing 11–3. This time, the Giants faced the Bears in the title game. New York got off to a better start. Tittle finally threw a touchdown pass in a championship game by hitting Gifford on a 14-yarder in the first quarter. The Giants took a 10–7 halftime lead. But Tittle came apart in the second half, throwing four interceptions as the Bears rallied to win 14–10.

The Giants had lost five title games in six seasons, and their players were getting older. In a controversial move, New York traded Huff to Washington after the 1963 season. Gifford retired

Linebacker Sam Huff (70) was named to the All-Pro team four times as a member of the Giants from 1956 to 1963.

Wide receiver and running back Joe Morrison spent his entire 14-season career with the Giants from 1959 to 1972.

after the 1964 season. New York couldn't recover. The team didn't have a winning record for the rest of the decade. Though the team's playoff runs were disappointing, many players realized later how strong the team was. "We represented the Giants," said defensive back Dick Lynch. "We took our shots, and we lost. But at least we were there at the end."

"WE TOOK OUR SHOTS, AND WE LOST. BUT AT LEAST WE WERE THERE AT THE END."

—DICK LYNCH

A NEW HOME

In 1970, the NFL merged with the American Football league and nearly doubled in size. The Giants joined many of the original NFL teams in the new National Football Conference (NFC). Meanwhile, in the 1966 season, the Super Bowl had been created to crown a league champion. Starting in the 1970 season, the game featured the best team in the NFC and the best in the American Football Conference (AFC).

But the Super Bowl was far from the minds of Giants fans. They just wanted a winning team again. Fans were also wondering where the team was going to play. From 1925 to 1955, the Giants had played in the Polo Grounds on the island of Manhattan. In 1956, they moved to Yankee Stadium in the nearby Bronx borough. But in 1973, the team's agreement with New York City ended.

The Mara family had long planned to build their own stadium. But with no room to build in New York City, the owners found a site across the Hudson River in East Rutherford, New Jersey. With the move to New Jersey happening in 1976, the Maras struck a new deal with Yale University in New Haven, Connecticut. For the 1973 and 1974 seasons, the Giants played their games 81 miles (130 km) away from New York City. The team had losing records both seasons. In 1975, the Giants returned to New York and spent a year at Shea Stadium, home to the city's other NFL team, the New York Jets. In 1976, the Giants officially moved to New Jersey. Many fans were upset that the team no longer played in New York. Though it was only 15 miles (24.1 km) from Yankee Stadium, East Rutherford was a world away for many Giants fans. Those who traveled to Giants Stadium were greeted with more losing football.

The Giants' lowest point came on November 19, 1978. The team was hosting the Philadelphia Eagles. In the final minute, the Giants had the ball and were up 17–12. Philadelphia had no timeouts, so

New York could simply snap the ball and take a knee to run out the clock. Instead, offensive coordinator Bob Gibson decided to call a running play. Quarterback Joe Pisarcik and running back Larry Csonka fumbled the exchange. Philadelphia defensive back Herm Edwards scooped up the ball and scampered 26 yards for the winning score. The play became known as "the Fumble" to Giants fans. As the team finished 6–10, it was just another reminder of how far the once-proud team had fallen.

Giants Stadium was the team's home from 1976 through 2009.

Giants quarterback Joe Pisarcik (9) watches Philadelphia Eagles defensive back Herm Edwards recover "the Fumble" in 1978.

Giants linebacker Lawrence Taylor recorded 142 sacks from 1981 to 1993.

CHAPTER 4

SUPER GIANTS

By 1981, the Giants had recorded only two winning seasons since 1964. A new player arrived that spring to help turn things around. With the second pick in the 1981 NFL Draft, New York selected linebacker Lawrence Taylor. Taylor was a fierce hitter who instantly became one of the most dominant defensive players in football.

Playing under defensive coordinator Bill Parcells, Taylor won both the Defensive Rookie of the Year and Defensive Player of the Year Awards that year. He recorded 133 tackles and helped the Giants reach a 9–7 record. Back in the playoffs, New York defeated the Philadelphia Eagles in the wild-card round before losing to the San Francisco 49ers in the divisional round.

Parcells once again changed New York's defensive formation. He used a 3–4 setup, with three linemen and four linebackers. Taylor played outside linebacker. Before he came along, most linebackers just reacted to the play in front of them. Taylor lined up to attack. Starting from a standing position, he used incredible speed to bolt at the snap and go after the quarterback. Few offensive linemen could stop him. Sacks became an official statistic in 1982, and Taylor spent the rest of his career racking them up. Playing alongside talented linebacker Harry Carson and linemen Jim Burt and Leonard Marshall, the Giants' defense became known as "the Big Blue Wrecking Crew." Legendary coach and broadcaster John Madden said of Taylor, "He changed the way defense is played."

A key member of "the Big Blue Wrecking Crew," linebacker Harry Carson (56) starred for the Giants from 1976 to 1988.

BILL AND PHIL

The Giants promoted Parcells to head coach in 1983. With a great defense, he just needed to get the offense up to speed. That meant getting the best out of quarterback Phil Simms, the team's top draft pick in 1979. Simms had struggled at times. After he missed the 1982 season with an injury, Parcells kept him on the bench to start 1983. A frustrated Simms wanted out of New York. He even said he hated playing for the demanding Parcells. But in October, Simms was injured and missed the rest of the season. The Giants won only three games without Simms. The then 28-year-old got his job back in 1984. He led New York to a 9–7 record and a playoff win.

Giants quarterback Phil Simms (11) gets instructions from coach Bill Parcells, *center*. The pair had a complicated relationship during their time together in New York.

By 1986, the Giants were a true contender. Running back Joe Morris set a team record with 1,516 rushing yards. The Big Blue Wrecking Crew allowed only 14.8 points per game.

Simms and Parcells still weren't close, but they managed to get along as the team went 14–2. Simms sent the ball to several receivers, but his favorite target was Mark Bavaro, who caught 66 passes. The 6-foot-4 tight end was tough to bring down once he had the ball.

NEARLY PERFECT

In the playoffs, the Giants' defense kicked into high gear. During two playoff games, they allowed only three points. New York rolled into Super Bowl XXI to face the Denver Broncos.

New York tight end Mark Bavaro fights through a tackle against the Denver Broncos in Super Bowl XXI on January 25, 1987.

Simms had been solid during the season, but he completed only 55.3 percent of his passes. Against Denver, he was nearly flawless. On New York's first drive, Simms completed six straight passes, including a 6-yard touchdown to tight end Zeke Mowatt. By the end of the first half, Simms was 12-of-15, but the Giants trailed 10–9.

In the second half, New York's defense shut down star Denver quarterback John Elway. And Simms couldn't miss. He completed all 10 of his passes. Even when his pass early in the fourth quarter bounced off Bavaro's normally sure hands, wide receiver Phil McConkey caught the deflection for a touchdown.

THE GATORADE SHOWER

After a big win over Washington in 1984, Giants' lineman Jim Burt dumped a cooler of Gatorade on coach Bill Parcells's head. The move was playful payback for Parcells criticizing Burt during the week leading up to the game. "The Gatorade Shower" was soon a Giants' tradition. And after linebacker Harry Carson dunked the coach at the end of Super Bowl XXI in January 1987, other teams had already picked up on it. It has become one of the most recognizable victory celebrations in sports.

In the end, Simms set a Super Bowl record by completing 88 percent of his passes. He also threw three touchdowns as the Giants won 39–20. For the first time in 30 years, the Giants were on top of the NFL.

THE PLAN

The Giants' time at the top didn't last long. In the three seasons after winning the Super Bowl, New York reached the playoffs only once and didn't win a postseason game. But in 1990, the Big Blue Wrecking Crew led the team back. Under the guidance of defensive coordinator Bill Belichick, the Giants allowed the fewest points in the league and finished 13-3.

Late in the season, the team's chances took a big hit when Simms broke his foot in a Week 15 loss to the Buffalo Bills. Jeff Hostetler stepped in at quarterback. Hostetler had been with the team since 1984, but he had played so little that he once considered quitting football. With the defense going strong in the playoffs, Hostetler just had to limit his mistakes. New York crushed the Chicago Bears 31-3 in the divisional round, then traveled to San Francisco to take on the 49ers in the NFC title game.

San Francisco had won the previous two Super Bowls, but the Giants weren't intimidated. The teams battled for 60 minutes. Many players called it the most physical game they ever played. In the fourth quarter, both Hostetler and San Francisco star quarterback Joe Montana left the game due to heavy hits. Montana didn't return, but Hostetler was back on the field to lead the Giants in the final moments. With the Giants trailing 13-12, Taylor recovered a fumble. New York

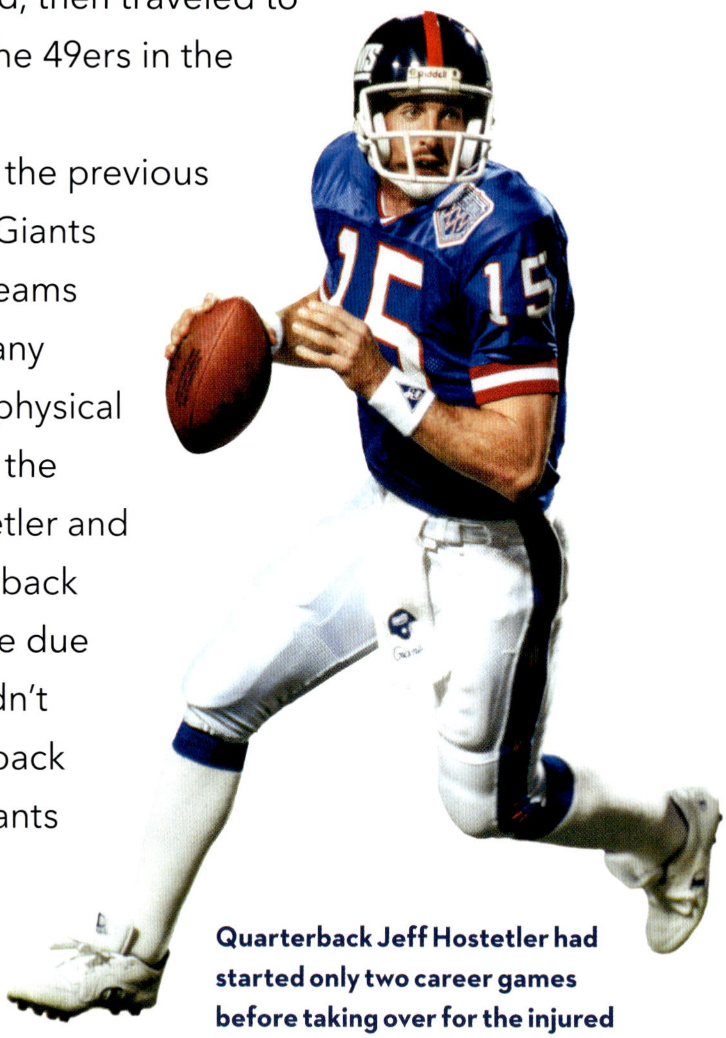

Quarterback Jeff Hostetler had started only two career games before taking over for the injured Simms late in the 1990 season.

drove down the field before kicker Matt Bahr hit his fifth field goal of the day. The Giants won 15-13.

The AFC-champion Bills were waiting for New York in the Super Bowl. Buffalo had one of the league's top offenses, relying on quick work and a three-receiver lineup to beat teams. To shut down Buffalo, Belichick drew up a surprising game plan. He often rushed Bills quarterback Jim Kelly with only two players. That left the other nine defenders available to smother Buffalo's receivers.

The Giants did their best to hold off Buffalo's potent offense. But Buffalo led 12–3 late in the first half. New York put together a scoring drive in the final minutes of the second quarter to pull

Kicker Matt Bahr gets a hug from Taylor as they celebrate alongside Hostetler after Bahr's game-winning kick in the NFC title game on January 20, 1991.

within two. The Giants then got the second-half kickoff. Leaning on running back Ottis Anderson, New York held the ball for nine minutes and 29 seconds. Anderson finished off the 14-play drive with a 1-yard touchdown plunge for a 17–12 lead. The game was hardly over, though. Buffalo scored early in the fourth quarter to go up 19–17, and then the Giants responded with another seven-minute drive capped by a field goal by Bahr.

Running back Ottis Anderson rushed for 102 yards and a touchdown during Super Bowl XXV on January 27, 1991.

New York still held a 20–19 lead in the final seconds, but Kelly maneuvered the Bills into position for a game-winning 47-yard field goal. In one of the most dramatic Super Bowl finishes ever, Buffalo kicker Scott Norwood pushed his kick wide

Giants players carry Parcells off the field after the team wins Super Bowl XXV.

to the right. The jubilant Giants flooded the field to celebrate their second Super Bowl title.

THE GUARANTEE

New York's victory in Super Bowl XXV marked the end of an era for the team. Parcells left after the season. Taylor and Simms both played three more years. The Giants spent the first half of the 1990s struggling to get back to the playoffs. Under new coaches

Ray Handley and then Dan Reeves, the team reached the postseason only once in six years.

In 1997, New York hired Jim Fassel as head coach. Though he was a former offensive coordinator, Fassel built his first Giants team around a strong defense. Defensive end Michael Strahan had become the team's fierce pass rusher. Cornerback Jason Sehorn was one of the best athletes in football. The Giants improved from 6–10 the previous year to 10–5–1 and won the NFC East title. But facing the Minnesota Vikings in the playoffs, New York blew a 22–13 lead in the final 90 seconds and lost 23–22. Fassel's Giants then missed the playoffs the next two years. By the start of the 1999 season, Fassel looked like another coach who wouldn't be able to get out of Parcells's shadow.

"THIS TEAM IS GOING TO THE PLAYOFFS."

—JIM FASSEL

New York started the 2000 season 7–2, but when the team lost back-to-back games, many wondered whether the Giants were about to collapse. After the second loss, Fassel addressed the media and made a bold claim: "This team is going to the playoffs," he said.

The Giants players rallied around their coach's words. New York won its final five games to top the division. Then the Giants knocked off the Eagles in the divisional round to set up a rematch with the Vikings for the NFC title.

Seeking revenge for the 1997 playoffs, New York was relentless. Playing in front of the home crowd, quarterback Kerry Collins threw a 46-yard touchdown pass to receiver Ike Hilliard on the game's first drive. The Giants then forced a fumble on the next kickoff, setting

New York fullback Greg Comella makes a falling touchdown catch in the first quarter of the NFC title game on January 14, 2001.

up another touchdown pass. New York led 14–0 before Minnesota had even run an offensive play.

The Giants' defense made sure there was no Vikings comeback. New York picked off Minnesota quarterback Daunte Culpepper three times and held the Vikings to just 114 yards. Collins finished the 41–0 rout with five touchdown passes.

The Giants' incredible turnaround took them all the way to Super Bowl XXXV. However, that brought a matchup with the Baltimore Ravens, who boasted one of the toughest defenses in NFL history. The Ravens' defense was just as fierce in the big game. New York's offense failed to score a touchdown. A kick return by receiver Ron Dixon accounted for the Giants' only points in a 34–7 loss.

Giants tight end Jeremy Shockey grabbed a second-quarter touchdown catch in the playoff game against the San Francisco 49ers on January 5, 2003.

CHAPTER 5

CINDERELLA GIANTS

AFTER A 10–6 SEASON IN 2002, THE GIANTS BUILT A 38–14 lead late in the third quarter of their playoff opener. But the San Francisco 49ers came roaring back to take the lead. With seconds remaining, New York lined up for a potential game-winning field goal. The snap was bad, and the Giants botched the play. New York's 39–38 loss marked one of the biggest collapses in NFL playoff history. The Giants wouldn't make the postseason again under Jim Fassel. After falling to 4–12 in 2003, the team fired Fassel.

TOUGH LOVE

The Giants brought back Tom Coughlin. As an assistant coach for New York, Coughlin had helped lead the team to a Super Bowl victory after the 1990 season. But Coughlin left after that win and later became the Jacksonville Jaguars' head coach. During his tenure in Jacksonville, Coughlin had developed a reputation as a stern taskmaster. No coach had more rules than "Tom the Tyrant." And he expected his players to follow them to the letter.

The Giants also had a brand-new quarterback. New York held the fourth pick in the 2004 draft. Most expected quarterback Eli Manning to go first overall to the San Diego Chargers. However, the younger brother of NFL star Peyton Manning said he didn't want to play for the Chargers. So New York and San Diego worked out a deal to swap picks, and Eli Manning headed to the Big Apple.

Manning's play was brilliant and erratic. He had a strong arm and good leadership abilities, but he often forced passes, leading to interceptions. Just like Manning, the Giants were an inconsistent team in Coughlin's first few years. They seemed capable of winning any game but often suffered head-scratching losses.

STRAHAN'S CONTROVERSIAL RECORD

On the final day of the 2001 season, Michael Strahan brought down Green Bay Packers quarterback Brett Favre late in the fourth quarter. The sack brought Strahan's total to 22 1/2 on the season, setting a new league record. The play was controversial, however, as Favre appeared to change the play to make sure Strahan got the sack. The old record holder, the New York Jets' Mark Gastineau, said later that he wanted Strahan's record back.

Defensive end Michael Strahan makes his record-setting sack on Green Bay Packers quarterback Brett Favre on January 6, 2002.

The fiery Tom Coughlin had been an assistant coach with the Giants from 1988 to 1990 before returning to the team as head coach in 2004.

In Coughlin and Manning's first three years, the team reached the playoffs twice but failed to win a postseason game.

Even worse, the players were turning on the stern Coughlin. Many hated playing for him. Running back Tiki Barber, the team's all-time leading rusher, retired at just 31 years old partly to avoid Coughlin. In 2007, Coughlin was about to be fired. Instead, owner John Mara told the coach to ease up.

Coughlin took his boss's advice, and the team responded. The Giants lost their first two games in 2007 but rebounded to finish 10–6. While Manning led the league with 20 interceptions, he also forged a strong bond with receiver Plaxico Burress, who caught 12 of Manning's 23 touchdowns. Running backs Brandon Jacobs and Derrick Ward filled in nicely for Barber. Meanwhile, star defensive end Michael Strahan, the team's emotional leader, led a strong pass rush alongside Osi Umenyiora and Justin Tuck.

GIANT KILLERS

The Giants entered the playoffs needing to win three road games to reach the Super Bowl. They took care of the first two with tough wins over the Tampa Bay Buccaneers and the Dallas Cowboys. That set up a trip to freezing Green Bay to take on the Packers in the NFC title game.

Giants' kicker Lawrence Tynes missed a potential game-winning field goal at the end of regulation. The struggling kicker was saved when defensive back Corey Webster intercepted Green Bay's star quarterback Brett Favre and returned the ball to the Packers' 34.

Kicker Lawrence Tynes celebrates his game-winning overtime field goal against the Green Bay Packers in January 2008.

Four plays later, Tynes got another chance. He drilled a 47-yard kick to send New York to Super Bowl XLII.

The Giants were a great success story, but the football world was sure their run was about to end. Waiting in Phoenix for the big game were the 18–0 New England Patriots. Led by quarterback Tom Brady, the Patriots were seeking to become the NFL's first perfect team since 1972. The Patriots had already won three Super Bowls since 2001 and boasted a record-setting offense.

The Giants surprised the football world by frustrating Brady and New England's offense. Tuck had two sacks as New York brought Brady down five times. But with 2:42 left, the Patriots' quarterback hit star receiver Randy Moss on a 6-yard touchdown pass to put New England up 14–10. Manning and the offense had struggled all game. With 1:15 left, the Giants faced third-and-seven at their own 44. Manning dropped back and was nearly swallowed up by the charging Patriots' defensive line. It looked as if Manning was about to go down, but he escaped. Rolling right, he heaved a pass down the middle of the field.

Few had heard of David Tyree before the Super Bowl. The receiver had only four catches all season. However, he had caught New York's first touchdown pass earlier in the fourth quarter, and now he leaped to grab another key catch. He got his hands on the ball at the same time as New England safety Rodney Harrison. As they fell, Tyree managed to pin the ball to his helmet and hold on.

Wide receiver David Tyree clutches the ball for his famous "Helmet Catch."

Strahan flexes his muscles after taking down New England's Tom Brady in Super Bowl XLII on February 2, 2008.

"The Helmet Catch" was an instant sensation and is still seen as one of the Super Bowl's all-time most exciting plays. Four plays later, Manning made the amazing moment count by lobbing a 13-yard touchdown pass to Burress. The defense held once more, and the Giants were shocking champions. After the game, Mara said, "It's the greatest victory in the history of this franchise, without question."

"IT'S THE GREATEST VICTORY IN THE HISTORY OF THIS FRANCHISE, WITHOUT QUESTION."

—JOHN MARA

ANOTHER UPSET

After pulling the incredible upset against New England, the Giants returned to being unpredictable. The team won the NFC East in 2008 but lost its playoff opener. After missing the postseason for the next two years, Coughlin was under pressure again.

In 2011, the Giants started 6–2, then stumbled to a 9–7 record. They managed to squeak into the playoffs, then started another run. After routing the Atlanta Falcons and the Packers in the first two rounds, Tynes played hero again in the NFC title game. His 31-yard field goal in overtime knocked off the 49ers and sent the Giants back to the Super Bowl.

Once again, they faced the Patriots. While New England wasn't undefeated, Brady's team was still considered the favorite. As was the case in Super Bowl XLII, both teams clamped down on defense. But the Patriots held a 17–9 lead in the third quarter before two field goals by Tynes tightened the score.

It was still 17–15 with 3:46 to go when the Giants took over at their own 12. With one last chance, the team went big on the first play. Manning dropped back and lobbed a pass aimed at receiver Mario Manningham down the left sideline. Manningham had one defender on his right hip and another racing over from the middle of the field. Manning's pass perfectly split the two defenders, and Manningham made the catch and got two feet down inbounds for a 38-yard gain.

The incredible throw and catch got the Giants moving. With 1:04 left, they had the ball at the New England 6. Patriots coach Bill Belichick decided to let New York score a touchdown so his offense could have a shot at a game-winning field goal. As Giants' running back Ahmad Bradshaw took off up the middle, the Patriots' defenders got out of his way. Realizing he didn't want to actually get into the end zone with so much time left, Bradshaw tried to stop at the 1. But he couldn't halt his momentum and ended up falling into the end zone for a 21–17 Giants lead.

Wide receiver Mario Manningham makes his 38-yard catch late in Super Bowl XLVI on February 5, 2012.

New York's defense needed to pull out one final stop. With five seconds left, Brady heaved a Hail Mary pass from the Patriots 49. Giants safety Kenny Phillips managed to escape the pack of players and swat the ball down. New York had beaten the odds again and became a four-time Super Bowl champion.

Running back Ahmad Bradshaw bursts through an open hole to score the winning touchdown in Super Bowl XLVI.

GIANTS TROPHY CASE

SUPER BOWL CHAMPIONSHIPS: 4

Super Bowl XXI - January 25, 1987
Super Bowl XXV - January 27, 1991
Super Bowl XLII - February 3, 2008
Super Bowl XLVI - February 5, 2012

NFL CHAMPIONSHIPS: 4

1927, 1934, 1938, 1956

CONFERENCE CHAMPIONSHIPS: 5

1986, 1990, 2000, 2007, 2011

DIVISION TITLES: 21

NFL East: 1933, 1934, 1935, 1938, 1939, 1941, 1944, 1956, 1958, 1959, 1961, 1962, 1963
NFC East: 1986, 1989, 1990, 1997, 2000, 2005, 2008, 2011

All stats are through the 2024 season.

Dexter Lawrence has been one of the NFL's top defensive tackles since the Giants drafted him with the 17th pick in the 2019 draft.

GIANT EXPECTATIONS

As they had in 2007, the Giants couldn't make their Super Bowl success last. Over the next 13 seasons, New York reached the postseason twice and won only one playoff game. After Coughlin's third straight losing season in 2016, the coach stepped aside. Manning retired four years later, having rewritten New York's passing record books.

With their championship pieces gone, the Giants searched for the next round of great players to continue the team's proud tradition. While stars such as disruptive defensive lineman Dexter Lawrence and receiver Malik Nabers provided thrills, the team still struggled. Representing the country's largest city in front of passionate Giants fans, New York's players looked to meet the expectations of the team's decorated past.

TIMELINE

1925
The Giants are founded by owner Tim Mara.

1934
The Giants win "the Sneakers Game" 30-13 over the Chicago Bears to secure the NFL championship.

1938
The Giants win the NFL Championship Game 23-17 over the Green Bay Packers.

1953
Longtime coach Steve Owen resigns and is replaced by Jim Lee Howell, who works with coordinators Vince Lombardi and Tom Landry.

1956
The Giants rout the Bears 47-7 to win the NFL title game.

1958
The Giants lose out on the NFL title game in overtime in "the Greatest Game Ever Played" against the Baltimore Colts.

1962
Giants quarterback Y. A. Tittle ties the NFL record by throwing seven touchdown passes in a single game.

1976
The Giants move to their new home in East Rutherford, New Jersey.

1987
New York wins its first Super Bowl title on January 25 by beating the Denver Broncos 39–20.

1991
On January 27, the Giants win Super Bowl XXV 20–19 over the Buffalo Bills.

2008
New York upsets the previously undefeated New England Patriots 17–14 on February 3 in Super Bowl XLII.

2012
On February 5, the Giants beat the Patriots 21–17 for New York's fourth Super Bowl title.

2024
The Giants select wide receive Malik Nabers with the sixth pick in the draft.

GLOSSARY

contender—a person or team that has a good chance at winning a championship.

coordinator—an assistant coach who is in charge of the offense, defense, or special teams.

draft—a system that allows teams to acquire new players coming into the league.

erratic—prone to making mistakes.

franchise—an entire sports organization.

general manager—an executive who runs a team and is responsible for finding and signing players.

Hail Mary—a long pass that has a small chance of succeeding, usually made near the end of a game as a last-ditch effort to score.

innovative—having new ideas about how something can be done.

merge—join with another to create something new, such as a company, a team, or a league.

momentum—the strength or force that allows something to continue or to grow stronger.

postseason—another word for playoffs; the time after the end of the regular season when teams play to determine a champion.

prospect—an athlete likely to succeed at the next level.

retire—to end one's career.

rival—an opponent with whom a player or team has a fierce and ongoing competition.

rookie—a professional athlete in his or her first year of competition.

sack–a tackle of the quarterback behind the line of scrimmage before he can pass the ball.

training camp–a set of practices held before the season to prepare for competition.

veteran–someone who has played for many years.

wild-card–the first round of the playoffs.

ONLINE RESOURCES

Booklinks
NONFICTION NETWORK
FREE! ONLINE NONFICTION RESOURCES

To learn more about the New York Giants, please visit **abdobooklinks.com** or scan this QR code. These links are routinely monitored and updated to provide the most current information available.

INDEX